Published in Great Britain in MMXXII by
The Salariya Book Company Ltd
25 Marlborough Place, Brighton BN1 1UB
www.salariya.com

ISBN: 978-1-913971-23-6

A CIP catalogue record for this book is available
from the British Library.

Printed and bound in Malta.

Author: John Townsend
Illustrator: Rory Walker
Editor: Nick Pierce

Visit
www.salariya.com
for our online catalogue and
free fun stuff.

The TV crew and television show in this book are works
of fiction. Names, characters, businesses, places, events,
locales and incidents are either the products of the
author's imagination or used in a fictitious manner.
Any resemblance to actual persons, TV crews or
television shows in the present or the past, or actual
events, is purely coincidental. The ghosts are all real!

LIVE FROM THE CRYPT ™

Interviews with the Ghosts of

Pirates

Series created by
David Salariya

Written by
John Townsend

Illustrated by
Rory Walker

SALARIYA
Brilliant Books Make Brilliant Children

LIVE FROM THE CRYPT

Meet the cast
TV crew:

MISH VARMA: HOST OF *LIVE FROM THE CRYPT* TV SHOW

JONTY YARDLEY: CO-HOST OF *LIVE FROM THE CRYPT* TV SHOW

LARNA OBATA: REPORTER

MANDY: HAIR & MAKE-UP

BINTI: DIRECTOR

KEV: CAMERA OPERATOR

ALEEMA: NEWSREADER

DUNCAN: SPECIAL CORRESPONDENT

GAIL FORSE: WEATHER PRESENTER

PROFESSOR PUDDLEWORTH: MARITIME HISTORIAN

Ghost Guests:

BLACKBEARD (C. 1680–1718): PIRATE CAPTAIN OF *QUEEN ANNE'S REVENGE*

MARY ORMOND (C. 1702–C. 1759): BLACKBEARD'S WIFE

CAPTAIN KIDD (C.1645–1701): PIRATE

SARAH KIDD (C. 1665–1744): WIFE OF CAPTAIN KIDD

HENRY MORGAN (1635–1688): PIRATE

MARY READ (C. 1695–1721): PIRATE

ANNE BONNY (C. 1698–C. 1782): PIRATE

CALICO JACK (1682–1720): ANNE'S PIRATE HUSBAND

LADY KILLIGREW (BEFORE 1525–1587): PIRATE

SAMUEL BELLAMY (C. 1689–1717): PIRATE

RACHEL WALL (1760–1789): PIRATE

BENJAMIN HORNIGOLD (1680–1719): PIRATE/PIRATE HUNTER

CAPTAIN ROBERT MAYNARD (1684–1751): PIRATE HUNTER

Contents

Introduction 7
Welcome to the programme 11
No script at the ship 21
Comic strip 1: How it all began 28
Behind the scenes 33
Comic strip 2: Blackbeard rules the waves 44
Commercial break 48
Comic strip 3: Robin Hood of the Sea – Samuel Bellamy 52
Forecast 57
Sail of the century (quiz show) 63
Comic strip 4: Fearsome female pirates 72
In a nutshell 77
Comic strip 5: Blackbeard meets his match 86
How nice to meet you 91
Comic strip 6: Pirate punishments 104
Ghosts reunited 109
Comic strip 7: Bartholomew Roberts gets it in the neck 116
Spin the news 121
Comic strip 8: Ching Shih and the Red Flag fleet 128
Sink or swim 133
For the wreck-ord 151
Family tree 158
Timeline 160
Quiz – Who wants to be a privateer? 164
Glossary 169
Live from the Crypt – In the classroom 170
Index 176

Introduction

Just imagine it... the TV crew arrives on location on board *The Cryptic*, a studio boat with its own submersible vessel. Connected by satellite to crypts around the world, the boat is moving north eastwards from the islands of the Caribbean to the coast of the USA. Wrecks of pirate ships lie sprawled on the seabed from South Carolina to Massachusetts, where the ghosts of pirates and their victims are often said to stir in their watery graves.

These ghosts have never been interviewed on live TV before and the wonders of the latest cutting-edge technology could just make this possible. How could ghosts with dramatic stories to tell refuse the invitation to talk on camera?

What if *The Cryptic*'s deck-manager, tea boy, technicians, make-up team, reporters, presenters and director are all waiting nervously for a 'live encounter with the dead'?

What if we switch on at home for the TV show they said could never be done: *Live from the Crypt*?

Sit back and dare to be stunned...

Stand-by for lights, cameras, music —

ACTION...

Welcome to the programme

MISH:

Hello and welcome to another of our crypt programmes coming to you live...

JONTY:

With a few dead ingredients – in our new series *Live from the Crypt.*

MISH:

With Jonty Yardley and me, Mish Varma.

JONTY:

Your ghost-hunters searching for some of the most famous ghosts in history.

MISH:

And tonight, we're coming 'live from the wreck' in the hope of meeting some of the real pirates of the Caribbean from 300 or more years ago, who plundered sailing ships on these very seas, in their hunt for treasure, riches and victims.

JONTY:

Victims? Are you sure we're safe?

MISH:

Of course. Our director is a dab hand at judo, jujitsu and origami. So if we're lucky, we might get an interview with one of the most feared pirates of all time.

JONTY:

That's right – the one with pistols, fireworks, swords and a fearsome beard.

MISH:

And we'll be meeting those who tried to hunt him down – and succeeded.

JONTY:

We are just approaching the site of his wrecked ship *Queen Anne's Revenge* that was discovered down there on the seabed in 1996 in the shallow waters of Beaufort Inlet here in North Carolina.

MISH:

Where the remains – and ghost – of the infamous Blackbeard are said to dwell.

JONTY:

Until we invite him up here onto our studio boat, *The Cryptic*, where we hope to interview him and ask about pirates, his lifestyle and maybe about pet parrots.

MISH:

Did he really have parrots on his ship?

JONTY:

Have you never heard of 'Parrots of the Caribbean'?
See what I did there?

MISH:

Moving on... Further north along the coast from
here on the shores of Cape Cod in Massachusetts,
archaeologists recently came across America's
largest mass pirate burial ground, containing over
100 pirates who washed up after their ship, the
Whydah, sank in 1717.

JONTY:

We'll be going next to that wreck, where the pirate
Samuel Bellamy, known as the Robin Hood of the
Sea, sank to the depths with his ship. We hope his
ghost will join us right here on the *Live from the
Crypt* sofa. Wouldn't that just be so awesome?

MISH:

Indeed – and a little damp. We'll need some towels
and a drip tray.

JONTY:

It was about forty years ago when divers

discovered Bellamy's wreck and it was the first authenticated pirate vessel ever to be discovered in North America.

MISH:

That's right, Jonty – and for those pirate buffs watching, you may know that Samuel Bellamy had a close connection with the fearsome Blackbeard.

JONTY:

That's because they once sailed on the same ship under the command of Benjamin Hornigold. They should have a lot to talk about.

MISH:

Unless they get violent and start swashbuckling all over the place.

JONTY:

Have we done a risk assessment? What happens if they take me hostage?

MISH:

We keep filming. What great telly that would be.

JONTY:

I hope they won't be armed.

MISH:

No, but you might get arrrrrmed. See, I can do daft pirate jokes, too.

JONTY:

I see what you did there – talking like a pirate.

MISH:

Actually, Jonty, no one really knows how pirates spoke. The 'Ooo arrrr' stuff just grew out of Hollywood and Disney films. It's all made-up.

JONTY:

So why are actors always talking like that when they act as pirates?

MISH:

Who knows?

JONTY:

They just arrrrr! See what I did there?

MISH:

It's time to move on. We'll be meeting pirates later who talk Scottish, Welsh, Irish, American and even posh. Several women were pirates and we're hoping to meet some of their ghosts tonight, as well as one of Blackbeard's wives. So be prepared for anything on tonight's show.

JONTY:

It's all very exciting, as we drop anchor above the wreck of *Queen Anne's Revenge* that was sunk in 1718. Some say Blackbeard's headless body swam down there to rest in peace after he was killed in battle.

MISH:

Let's hope we'll soon find him when our on-the-spot reporter descends to the wreck-site any time now in our special submersible vessel.

JONTY:

Then let's go live to Larna, who is below us and hoping to meet the wreck's scary ghost sometime soon. I can see on our screen the view from her submarine.

MISH:

> I think I saw a shadowy figure disappear into the wreck just ahead.

JONTY:

> Just a head? Let's hope we can find the rest of him. See what I did there?

MISH:

> No, Jonty. We hope Blackbeard will want to come up here and join us on our sofa on our floating set in this exclusive *Live from the Crypt* outside broadcast.

JONTY:

> Yes, and we're connected to several crypts tonight in Britain and America, where our cameras are waiting at the graves of pirates who sailed these waters in what is now known as 'the golden age of piracy'. But first up, let's see what pictures are coming up from far below us on the seabed.

MISH:

> Yes, Jonty – our special cameras and lights are scouring the wreck, as Larna steers the minisub

around the ship's eerie hull and gun deck packed with rusting cannons and the crumbling bones of pirates...

JONTY:

I can already hear in my earpiece that Larna is sensing a presence. Let's hope it's not a shark on the lookout for TV reporters.

MISH:

It's time to be serious, Jonty. We need to stop talking and let Larna see what develops – totally unscripted.

JONTY:

(whispering) So we now join Larna LIVE for 'No script at the crypt'. We're gripped! Or 'On deck at the wreck'. We're high-tech – let's check...

No Script at the Ship

LARNA:

(*Whispering*) I'm down here in the dark and spooky depths of the wreck. I am steering around the smashed masts covered in seaweed, where fish dart among the crusty cannons. Now I'm passing the rudder and peering into what looks like the captain's cabin where I can see broken beams and...

VOICE:

Go away.

LARNA:

I think I heard a voice. I'll extend the ultra-sensitive waterproof microphone and I'll talk into the audio system. Is that Captain Blackbeard, by any chance?

BLACKBEARD:

Well it's not Mary, Queen of Scots, is it? What do you want?

LARNA:

We're 'Live from the Wreck' hoping to meet you and Samuel Bellamy.

BLACKBEARD:

Pah – him! At least I went down fighting, whereas he and his crew went down in a storm a year before my final battle. I was a better sailor than him.

LARNA:

Well, maybe you'd like to discuss that with him if he joins us...

BLACKBEARD:

I don't discuss, I fight. Do you want to see us have a good old swashbuckle?

LARNA:

No – just a friendly chat. Tell us about being one of the most feared pirates of all time. You had a terrifying reputation.

BLACKBEARD:

That was my secret. If enemies dreaded meeting me, I was top-dog from the start. They'd just give up and hand over their stuff without a fight. Job done.

LARNA:

Apparently you wove strands of rope into your bushy beard and set it on fire when you attacked a ship. Your smoky face scared sailors so much they ran and fled.

BLACKBEARD:

It never failed. I haven't tried that trick for years. It's not easy lighting fuses underwater with a soggy beard and a head that falls off when I roar like a tiger.

LARNA:

I'm sure we can do something to fix it when we go on air.

BLACKBEARD:

On hair? You leave my hair alone. My wife loved my beard and hair.

LARNA:

We're hoping to meet her, too. Is it true you had several wives?

BLACKBEARD:

It's none of your business. I never discuss my private life.

LARNA:

That's a shame because the world doesn't know much about you. We think your real name is Edward Teach or Thatch.

BLACKBEARD:

My name is the same as my father's – Edward Thache. He sailed ships and moved to Bristol, the English shipping port, when he married. After my sister and I were born, our mother died so he married again and had three more children. I don't know why I'm telling you all this, it's none of your business.

LARNA:

But can I persuade you to come up to our boat and talk to us more so you can put the record straight? After all, there are many myths about you.

BLACKBEARD:

Like what?

LARNA:

That you buried treasure because you were scared of other pirates getting it. And you weren't the most successful pirate around, were you?

BLACKBEARD:

Rubbish! Right – it's time for me to get up there and tell it straight. I'll show you just how successful I was. Get ready for me to defend my reputation.

LARNA:

Brilliant, we'll have a world-exclusive interview! So whilst we wait for you to join us, it's back to Mish and Jonty on the sofa with their fingers firmly crossed...

MISH:

(Back on the sofa) It's sounding promising. And I've just heard we've got other ghost pirates lined up who want to talk.

JONTY:

I can't wait for them to arrrrrr-ive and aaaaarsk questions. See what I did there?

MISH:

No more pirate talk, Jonty.

JONTY:

Very well, Mish. Even though it's biz-arrrrre that Blackbeard's ghost is coming to spook to us. See what I did there? Before he joins us up here on the 'Live from the Wreck' sofa, let's take a look at our plasma screen storyboard to remind us about when he ruled in the golden age of piracy...

How it all began...

SPANISH GALLEONS KNOWN AS THE SPANISH TREASURE FLEET SAIL THE WORLD IN THE 16TH CENTURY.

IT'S A FLOATING TREASURE HOUSE READY FOR GRABBING.

WE CARRY BEAUTIFUL THINGS TO AND FROM THE AMERICAS FOR THE SPANISH EMPIRE.

BY THE 1570S, ENGLAND'S QUEEN ELIZABETH I SEES SPAIN AS A SERIOUS ENEMY.

SPAIN KEEPS GETTING RICHER. HOW ABOUT ROBBING SOME OF THEIR SHIPS?

I THINKEST ALL THIS GOLD AND SILVER MAKETH ME THE RICHEST SAILOR EVER. PRITHEE, HOW VERILY SPLENDID, METHINKS.

1579: CAPTAIN FRANCIS DRAKE DELIGHTS THE QUEEN BY SEIZING THE SPANISH TREASURE SHIP *NUESTRA SEÑORA DE LA CONCEPCIÓN*.

29

Behind the Scenes

BINTI:

There's still no sign of Blackbeard's ghost. We've lost communication with Larna in the sub so I've got no idea what's happening. As the director, I'm in a panic. We won't have a programme if no one shows up anytime soon.

KEV:

The deep-sea camera is only picking up weird and fuzzy images around the wreck. I can't see any pirates anywhere.

BINTI:

We'll have to go to a commercial break and get someone to dress up as Blackbeard. Mandy, as you do hair and make-up, you could easily make yourself look like a pirate ghost.

MANDY:

(Offended) In a black beard? I'd look ridiculous.

BINTI:

We could light fuses in it to make it smoke like Blackbeard used to do.

MANDY:

What about 'health and safety'? It's a bit risky.

BINTI:

You're right, Mandy – Kev will have to do it. Give him a big bushy beard and some firecrackers, quick. He'll have to pretend to be Blackbeard in jeans and talk in a scary pirate voice.

KEV:

I can't do voices. Anyway, who would work the camera?

BINTI:

I will. No, better still, let's play for time. Bring in that professor of maritime history who navigated us here. Meanwhile, tell Larna to get a move on. Hurry the ghost and get him here fast.

MANDY:

I don't want to do Blackbeard's makeup when he arrives. He'll look ever-so wrinkly after being underwater all that time and his beard might be full of crawly crabs and wriggly eels.

BINTI:

That's the least of my worries. We haven't got a programme.

KEV:

Yikes, I've just had a signal in my headphones. We've got ten seconds till our sofa goes live around the world.

BINTI:

Quick – Mish and Jonty stand by.

MISH:

What do we say?

KEV:

Seven seconds.

BINTI:

Make something up. Anything. Keep talking till someone shows up.

JONTY:

I can't waffle for long.

MISH:

You usually do.

KEV:

Three seconds... two... one...

MISH:

Welcome back to *Live From the Crypt* where we're anchored above the wreck of the *Queen Anne's Revenge* pirate ship that belonged to Blackbeard himself, whose ghost has been seen swirling around the decks.

JONTY:

And who, any minute now, will be joining us on

the sofa with a soggy beard and straggly hair... just as soon as he appears. We hope. Possibly. Perhaps.

MISH:

But in the meantime, we are joined by Professor Puddleworth, who knows all about the Golden Age of Piracy and the history of ships.

PROFESSOR:

(Rushing on) I wasn't expecting this. What do you want to know?

JONTY:

Just give us a few facts and figures about pirates from the days of Blackbeard.

PROFESSOR:

Well, Blackbeard's real name was Edward Thache and he was born around 1680 when pirates were already causing great problems. It was a time when French, Spanish, Dutch, English and Portuguese ships were not just trading around the world, but also colonising North and South America, including the Caribbean. The hideous slave trade was also underway, so sea traffic was growing fast. Many

of the new colonies were not properly governed and didn't have enough policing to protect them from pirate attacks.

MISH:

So this was a golden age if you happened to be a pirate who liked gold. It wasn't a good time for honest sailors or imprisoned slaves crossing the ocean.

JONTY:

With such huge amounts of valuable cargo being shipped over the oceans, I guess that European navies couldn't always protect them from rampaging pirates.

PROFESSOR:

To begin with, there just weren't enough navy ships. In fact, many experienced sailors were out of work and their best hope of making a living was to join a pirate ship. It was a violent and dangerous world and few pirates survived to old age.

MISH:

So jolly stories of friendly gentlemen pirates are just fiction, are they?

PROFESSOR:

Many pirates were ruthless murderers. Take Edward Low, a pirate of the 1720s in the Caribbean. He was one of the cruellest pirates ever, who delighted in torturing and killing his victims. If anyone upset him, Low thought nothing of inflicting slow and painful deaths to everyone onboard a ship whilst he laughed evilly.

JONTY:

Yuck, how low can you get. See what I did there?

MISH:

It's not a joking matter, Jonty. Moving on... how ruthless was Blackbeard?

PROFESSOR:

Some reports said his bark was worse than his bite and he didn't like hurting people at all. In fact, he apparently attacked slave ships, released the slaves and let them work for him as pirates!

MISH:

It was probably from the frying pan into the fire for them.

JONTY:

You mean he made them work in the galley as cooks?

MISH:

I was talking figuratively, Jonty.

JONTY:

What sort of figures?

PROFESSOR:

Many hundreds of pirates during the golden age of piracy would have been slaves from Africa. In the late 1600s and early 1700s, a pirate ship was one of the few places African people could earn good money in the Caribbean. For slaves it was often a better choice to become a pirate rather than suffer a life of slavery. Maybe up to one-third of 10,000 pirates at sea during the golden age of piracy were former slaves. Whilst many were still mistreated, some captains insisted on equality among their crew, regardless of race. We think Blackbeard was one of those who let African pirates vote, have their own weapons and receive an equal share of the booty. That was seen as a far better prospect than being resold into slavery.

MISH:

I find the slave trade totally sickening.

PROFESSOR:

Talking of sickening, life at sea for pirates was often full of sickness. Disease and injuries were common. Getting seasick was a serious occupational hazard.

JONTY:

Seasick? Surely not those tough, rugged pirates?

PROFESSOR:

Storms at sea could throw sailing ships on mountainous waves for days. They didn't just bob up and down gently like this boat we're on.

JONTY:

Please don't remind me, Professor. I'm trying not to think about it.

PROFESSOR:

I can feel it all the time sitting here... up and down, up and down, up and down...

JONTY:

Please don't... sorry about this – excuse me
(*rushing off*).

MISH:

In that case, we'd better move on to our next item...
whatever it is.

BINTI:

(*Through headphones*) Go to another storyboard or
something. Where's Larna? Hurry up with the ghost
– where is he? And will someone get Jonty's head
out of that bucket?

MANDY:

He looks very green. He'll need a lot of extra
make-up.

KEV:

Cue next storyboard screen: three, two, one...

Blackbeard rules the waves

DURING THE 1680s, THE THACHE FAMILY LEAVES BRISTOL FOR JAMAICA.

I'M GOING TO OWN A SUGAR PLANTATION.

I'M GOING TO EAT LOTS OF SUGAR.

I'M GOING TO DIE SOON.

I'M GOING TO GROW A BEARD ONE DAY.

YOUNG EDWARD THACHE JOINS THE ROYAL NAVY AND SERVES ABOARD *HMS WINDSOR* BASED AT PORT ROYAL, JAMAICA.

WE'RE FIGHTING FRENCH SHIPS TO STOP THEM GETTING CONTROL IN NORTH AMERICA. SO FAR I'VE HAD A FEW CLOSE SHAVES.

I CAN'T WAIT TO GROW A BEARD.

EDWARD SERVES IN QUEEN ANNE'S WAR BETWEEN ENGLAND AND FRANCE (1702–1713).

NOVEMBER 1717: EDWARD ATTACKS *LA CONCORDE*, A FRENCH SLAVE SHIP IN THE CARIBBEAN.

I'VE CAPTURED IT BY A WHISKER!

ALL SLAVES CAN JOIN MY CREW AS PIRATES. I SHALL BE KNOWN AS CAPTAIN BLACKBEARD.

I WONDER WHY...

EDWARD RENAMES THE SHIP *QUEEN ANNE'S REVENGE*.

IT'S A SKELETON WITH AN HOURGLASS – WARNING YOUR TIME IS ABOUT TO RUN OUT IF YOU DARE FIGHT ME.

CAPTAIN BLACKBEARD RAISES HIS OWN FLAG.

Commercial break

LOOKING FOR ADVENTURE?

GOOD AT SWASHBUCKLING?

KEEN ON HUNTING TREASURE?

THEN COME TO 'PIRATES ARRRRR US', THE SHIP-SHAPE
TRAVEL COMPANY THAT PROVIDES GREAT OPPORTUNITIES
TO VISIT THE GLORIOUS CARIBBEAN, LIE ON SUNNY DESERT
ISLANDS AND EVEN SWIM WITH SHARKS
(IF YOU UPSET THE CAPTAIN).

LEARN NEW SKILLS, MEET NEW FRIENDS, REACH NEW
DEPTHS. WHAT COULD BE BETTER THAN STROLLING THE
DECK OF A PIRATE SHIP IN COOL BLASTS OF SEA AIR IN
A REFRESHING HURRICANE? ENJOY FRIENDLY COMPANY –
ESPECIALLY SLEEPING WITH CUDDLY SHIP RATS, BEFORE
WAKING IN A COMFY HAMMOCK READY FOR A HIGH PROTEIN
BREAKFAST: MAGGOTY SHIP'S BISCUITS WASHED DOWN
WITH AS MUCH RUM AS YOU LIKE
(IT'S MUCH SAFER THAN DRINKING THE WATER).

The Ultimate Pirate Experience

ENJOY BOISTEROUS BANTER WITH OTHER JOLLY
PIRATES, WORLD FAMOUS FOR THEIR SENSE
OF FAIR PLAY, KINDNESS AND UTTER CHARM —
DESPITE SCURVY, FESTERING WOUNDS AND
GUT—WRENCHING SEASICKNESS. YES,
WE GUARANTEE EVERY DAY WILL BE AN
ADVENTURE YOU'LL NEVER FORGET.

'PIRATES ARRRRR US' - FOR AN EXPERIENCE
THAT'S TRULY SPECTACULARRRRR
(AND LIKELY YOUR LAST).

TERMS & CONDITIONS APPLY. PAU DISCLAIMS ALL
RESPONSIBILITY FOR LOSS OF LIMBS, SHARK ATTACKS OR
SAVAGE KIDNAPPING. SHOULD YOU CATCH SIGHT OF BLACKBEARD
OR HIS FLAG, YOU ARE ADVISED TO GIVE UP THE WILL TO
LIVE IMMEDIATELY. PAU CANNOT BE HELD RESPONSIBLE FOR
SEVERE TRAUMA, LIFE—THREATENING TORTURE OR ANY GROSS
ENCOUNTERS WITH A BLACK AND SMOULDERING SMELLY BEARD.

Sample Supper Menu

SQUID & SEA SNAKE BROTH PIE	£3
SEAGULL & JELLYFISH PIE	£4
SEAWEED PIE (VEGGIE OPTION)	£2
COCONUT & BARNACLE RUM PIE	£5
PARROT & SCALLOPS BRANDY PIE	£6

NB THESE PRICES ARE THE CURRENT
PIE RATES OF THE CARIBBEAN

Robin Hood of the Sea – Samuel Bellamy

SAMUEL BELLAMY IS BORN IN DEVON, ENGLAND AROUND 1689.

OO ARR.

OO ARR, I BE FIGHTING THE FRENCH IN QUEEN ANNE'S WAR.

IN HIS TEENS, BELLAMY JOINS THE BRITISH NAVY AND SAILS TO AMERICA.

HE JUMPS SHIP TO BECOME A TREASURE HUNTER.

WOW, THE FLORIDA COAST IS STUFFED WITH SUNKEN SPANISH TREASURE!

HE SOON JOINS BENJAMIN HORNIGOLD'S PIRATE CREW.

HOW DO I LOOK?

I'M THE COOLEST-LOOKING PIRATE EVER.

IN 1716, THE CREW REVOLT AND CHOOSE SAMUEL AS THEIR CAPTAIN.

Forecast

JONTY:

Whilst we're still waiting for Blackbeard to surface and for me to find my sea legs, we'll take a look at the weather forecast for the Caribbean in the early 1700s.

MISH:

So let's go over to Gail Forse. What sort of conditions could Blackbeard and all those pirates expect, Gail? What might be coming their way?

GAIL:

A good question, Mish. It looks like everything gets off to a good start, with plenty of fresh sea breezes to fill the sails and flutter the Jolly Roger flags around the seas off America. But that's until the hurricane season strikes between June and November, when the Caribbean and east coast of America can get very scary. And, of course, pirates in the 1700s have no idea when the next storm will strike. Here's a map of the pirate's favourite hunting area.

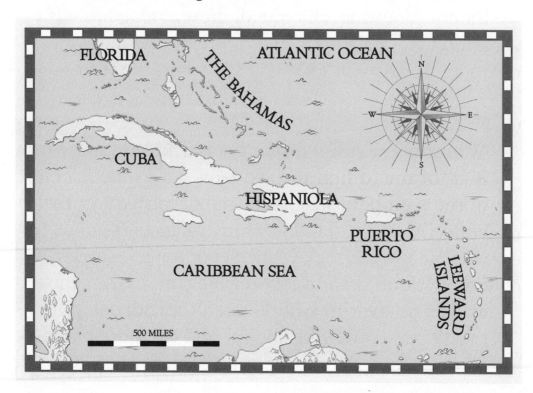

This part of the world is in the path of massive storms that can quickly smash sailing ships to pieces. From 1715 to 1720, more pirates are killed by bad weather than by navy guns or enemy swords. On 31st July 1715, a severe hurricane will strike the Florida coast (called the treasure coast because of all the wrecked treasure ships here). A fleet of 12 ships packed with treasure will leave Havana in Cuba and head into the Bahamas Channel. Three ships will sink in deep water and the rest will be swept onto the Florida coast and wrecked. More than a thousand sailors will drown, together with pirates caught in this one raging hurricane. Many more storms will follow in the months ahead.

A quick reminder...

A hurricane (tropical cyclone) is a large, rotating storm with high-speed winds that forms over warm waters in tropical areas. Hurricanes with winds of over 113 kilometres (70 miles) per hour, lashing rain and with an area of low air pressure in the centre called the eye can whip the sea into dangerously mountainous waves.

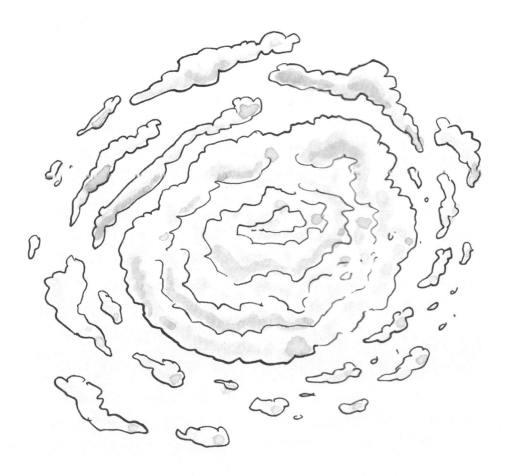

The very areas where pirates are known to operate
are at greatest risk of sudden storms. Indeed, plenty
of stormy times are just ahead, as pirates, sailors
and navies do battle here – not just with themselves,
but with all those hurricanes sweeping in.

We have to issue a severe warning that conditions will worsen soon, so be prepared for all sorts of trouble at sea in the 18th century and beyond. Just in case any pirates are watching, I would also remind you that this area contains the dreaded Bermuda Triangle – where anything can happen. Don't have nightmares, take care and good luck. And that's your forecast.

Sail of the century (quiz show)

JONTY:

Hello again – and whilst we're still waiting for Blackbeard to join us on the sofa, we've managed to link up to a grave in England. Isn't that so, Mish?

MISH:

Indeed, Jonty. We have a satellite link to a churchyard near Canterbury where the ghost of Captain Robert Maynard of the Royal Navy is ready to talk to us live.

JONTY:

Well, almost live. And he's agreed to take part in a quiz that I'm calling 'Sail of the century'. Sail, as in setting sail, as in ships. See what I did there? After all, Captain Maynard's heroic battle with pirates was surely one of the biggest sailing stories from the 18th century. It helped him get ahead from Lieutenant to Captain. And 'get a head' is just what he did. Blackbeard's head.

MISH:

Moving on... we now hand you over to Duncan, our quiz master, who will be asking Robert Maynard to sit in the spotlight and score some points. Over to you, Duncan.

DUNCAN:

Yes, welcome to my guest tonight, now known as Captain Maynard, who masterminded the defeat of Blackbeard and his pirate crew. He is about to take his place in the famous black chair...
(Lights lower, music, spotlight on chair)

MAYNARD:

Good evening.

DUNCAN:

You are Robert Maynard and what is your occupation?

MAYNARD:

Full time ghost. Former officer in the British Navy.

DUNCAN:

And what is your specialist subject?

MAYNARD:

Pirates and myself.

DUNCAN:

Captain Maynard, you have one minute to answer the following questions: You were an officer on *HMS Pearl*. What was your mission?

MAYNARD:

King George I sent the British Navy to prevent piracy off the American coast. I was asked by the Governor of Virginia to patrol the coast of North Carolina where the pirate Blackbeard was known to operate. My mission was to catch or kill him and his crew of ruthless pirates.

DUNCAN:

Correct. What was his notorious ship called?

MAYNARD:

Queen Anne's Revenge. She had 40 cannon and a crew of over 300 pirates.

DUNCAN:

Correct. Why did Blackbeard team up with other pirate ships in this area?

MAYNARD:

They all got together and blockaded the port of Charles Town in South Carolina. In other words, they sealed it off and held it to ransom. The inhabitants had to pay to let people or goods get through. It was despicable.

DUNCAN:

Correct. But Blackbeard himself was granted a royal what?

MAYNARD:

Pardon.

DUNCAN:

I said, 'Blackbeard was granted a royal what?'

MAYNARD:

Pardon. A royal pardon. If he promised to give up being a pirate, the king agreed to let him off. So Blackbeard settled down in Bath, North Carolina.

DUNCAN:

Correct. So if Blackbeard was no longer a threat, why did you go after him?

MAYNARD:

Pah! Once a pirate, always a pirate. He couldn't resist going back to his old ways, even though he'd run *Queen Anne's Revenge* into a sandbar. He now had a ship called *Adventure* and my spies told me it was anchored in the Ocracoke Inlet.

DUNCAN:

So you sneaked up on him?

MAYNARD:

Correct.

DUNCAN:

Oh good, now I've got a point. When did you finally track Blackbeard down?

MAYNARD:

22nd November 1718. It's etched on my mind forever.

DUNCAN:

Correct. So what happened next?

MAYNARD:

My two ships entered the channel but Blackbeard must have been on the lookout, doing a spot of naval-gazing. A blast ripped through us and killed many of my men. I commanded my crew to hide below deck to make Blackbeard think only a few of us were left. In that way, I lured him onto my deck where I stood my ground to do battle with him.

DUNCAN:

Correct. We won't give away what happened next but, enough to say, you were eventually made a captain.

MAYNARD:

Pah! Not for at least 20 years. And then all I got was a little monument in the church to say 'brave and gallant Actions in the Service of his King and Country. He retired to this place where he died 4 January 1751 aged 67'. I didn't even get a decent reward for risking life and limb.

DUNCAN:

Correct. Now, just some last quick-fire questions – if I can use that term to a naval officer. Firstly, when your ship attempted to overtake Blackbeard's, what were you trying to do?

MAYNARD:

Pass.

DUNCAN:

Correct. When you trained as a naval officer, what did you have to do?

MAYNARD:

Pass.

DUNCAN:

Correct. To navigate at sea, pirates would often stroke a nail over a magnetic rock called a lodestone to make it point north. This acted like a com...

MAYNARD:

Pass.

DUNCAN:

Correct. Different types of compass were used for centuries, of course. Pirates who unlawfully boarded someone else's ship were guilty of tres...

MAYNARD:

Pass.

DUNCAN:

Correct. Trespass is only one of their crimes... Now, I've started so I'll finish... Pirates who played games might wrap a gold bar in layers then send it from one to another till the music stopped. They called this 'something' the parcel. What?

MAYNARD:

Pass.

DUNCAN:

Correct. And at the end of that round, Captain Maynard, you have scored 12 points. After that impressive performance, you can now return to rest in peace whilst we visit again the giant plasma screen for the next pirate storyboard where we meet two of the fearsome female pirates of Blackbeard's time...

TWO SCARY WOMEN COMING UP...

Fearsome female pirates

MARY READ IS BORN AROUND 1685 IN ENGLAND.

YOUR HALF-BROTHER HAS DIED SO I'LL DRESS YOU AS HIM SO THAT WE STILL GET MAINTENANCE MONEY.

WHAT ARE YOU STARING AT? OF COURSE I'M A GUY.

MARY, KNOWN AS MARK, BECOMES A SAILOR IN HER TEENS.

YOU SEEM LIKE A TOUGH GUY, YOU CAN JOIN US.

SAILING TO THE CARIBBEAN, MARY IS CAPTURED BY PIRATES.

NO SWEAT - OO ARRR.

In a nutshell

MISH:

Welcome back. We're still waiting for our ghost to appear. Apparently it takes a long time for a bearded pirate to float to the surface. So we'll go over to our Special Correspondent who has been given a real challenge tonight.

JONTY:

Yes, Duncan has the tricky task in *Live from the Crypt* to make the big subject of 'piratey paraphernalia' as simple and short as possible – 'In a nutshell'.

MISH:

Not only does he have to keep us engaged, but he must also give us the basic facts in under a minute.

JONTY:

And Duncan has just been joined by Professor Puddleworth to explain some piracy terms and throw away some of the myths that have cluttered our thinking about the age of piracy. Over to you, Duncan, and good luck...

DUNCAN:

Yes, welcome to 'In a nutshell' and a special welcome to Professor Puddleworth.

PROFESSOR:

I'm happy to be back and to explain firstly some of the different types of pirates. The 'official' ones that worked for governments against enemy countries were known as privateers. They would rob foreign ships on behalf of their king or queen, whilst doubtless keeping some sparkly trinkets for themselves.

DUNCAN:

So who were Buccaneers? Weren't they much the same?

PROFESSOR:

Yes, but they were sailors who attacked ships in the Caribbean. Remember, islands of the West Indies were busy with trade, slaves and treasure in the 17th and 18th centuries. Buccaneers invented a special kind of weapon called a cutlass, which was a short, heavy sword with a curved blade – and scary. The Buccaneer Musket was a large and heavy gun that could shoot someone on an enemy deck 300 metres (984 feet) away.

DUNCAN:

So they were Caribbean privateers. Was another type of pirate called a corsair?

PROFESSOR:

Corsairs were just the same, but they sailed the southern shores of the Mediterranean Sea off North Africa. They also fought with curved swords, called scimitars, that were used when kidnapping victims before selling them as slaves.

DUNCAN:

Did they all fly flags showing the infamous skull and crossbones?

PROFESSOR:

Not necessarily. Some pirates preferred to use their own personal design for a flag. Where the name 'Jolly Roger' came from to refer to the skull and crossbones is unclear. As ships once flew red flags to warn 'no mercy will be given', the name may have come from the French 'Joli Rouge' ('pretty red') – or maybe the term used for the Devil: 'Old Roger'.

DUNCAN:

So what about all that stuff with eyepatches, earrings, wooden legs and parrots on shoulders? Did pirates really look like that?

PROFESSOR:

Very rarely! A lot of our modern ideas about pirates came from the Scottish writer Robert Louis Stevenson, who wrote *Treasure Island* in 1882. He invented a one-legged pirate called Long John Silver who had a parrot called Captain Flint which squawked 'pieces of eight'.

DUNCAN:

Wasn't that the money pirates used?

PROFESSOR:

Yes, pieces of eight were the world's first global currency. They were Spanish coins and were used across much of the world when Spain had a huge empire.

DUNCAN:

So why was it called pieces of eight?

PROFESSOR:

Back then it was legal to cut up coins into pieces. When people gave change, they literally cut the coins into eight pieces, or 'bits.' So British pirates called the Spanish dollar a 'piece of eight' – a coin worth eight pieces.

DUNCAN:

Back to the parrots and eyepatches... were they common on pirate ships?

PROFESSOR:

Hardly. Although there are some records of parrots being kept as pets on ships, very few pirates were likely to have one perched on the shoulder. And it's doubtful many wore eyepatches – either pirates or parrots!

DUNCAN:

But many wore earrings, didn't they?

PROFESSOR:

Maybe not many parrots did, but pirates often wore gold or silver earrings as a type of insurance to pay for their burial if they got killed. One thing pirates feared was dying at the bottom of the ocean, known as Davy Jones's Locker. They also dreaded being washed ashore without the funds for a decent burial. Some pirates even engraved the name of their home port on the inside of their earrings so that their bodies could be sent home for a proper burial. A few pirate graveyards have been found near some ports.

DUNCAN:

I wouldn't like to go near those after dark. Just one last question about ships. I get a bit confused by all the different types of sailing ships there used to be. Have the pirate movies got it right with how pirate ships looked?

PROFESSOR:

Pirates basically used all sorts of sailing ships. Don't think they all sailed in those enormous multi-decked armed galleons used by wealthy Europeans. Many pirates used whatever they could get, often smaller ships called galleys. These were long and narrow with banks of oars. Unlike the grand sailing ships that they attacked, galleys could be rowed against the wind and in any direction. Many pirates worked from sloops which were sleek, fast and good for sailing up alongside their bigger prey.

DUNCAN:

Fascinating stuff – and it's amazing how we're still hooked on pirate tales from the past. Maybe 'hooked' is the right word when it comes to pirate myths. Hooks and wooden legs are only the stuff of fiction, it seems.

PROFESSOR:

Mostly, but pirates themselves were scarily real and still are. Some operate in parts of the Pacific and Indian Oceans today. They cost the world billions of dollars a year. Modern pirates, like those of long ago, steal ships and their cargo, as well as kidnapping and injuring their victims. I can't say more as I've run out of time!

DUNCAN:

Indeed you have. It just remains for me to say thank you, Professor Puddleworth, for explaining all that in a nutshell and within 60 seconds. That gives us enough time to go back to the plasma screen storyboard to look at what happened when Blackbeard met Officer Maynard face to face for the battle of battles. Look away now if you're of a nervous disposition...

Blackbeard meets his match

BLACKBEARD'S REPUTATION SCARES SAILORS EVEN BEFORE THEY SEE HIM.

HAND OVER YOUR RICHES OR PERISH!

WAS IT SOMETHING I SAID?

AFTER 5 SHOTS, BLACKBEARD STAGGERS ACROSS THE DECK AND FALLS.
SAY GOODBYE TO YOUR HEAD, YOU WRETCH.
BLACKBEARD IS FINALLY KILLED, FOR ALL TO SEE.
THAT DIDN'T GO VERY WELL.

How nice to meet you

MISH:

Welcome back to the *Live from the Crypt* sofa with me, Mish Varma...

JONTY:

And me, Jonty Yardley – and we're very excited, aren't we, Mish?

MISH:

Excited and scared because finally, at last, our special ghost guest has just arrived on set and will be joining us on the sofa any minute.

JONTY:

Yes, the ghost of Blackbeard is just drying off and having his beard wrung out.

MISH:

The reason we're a little late meeting him is that we've had to drag him up from the wreck below, pop him under the dryer and iron out his crinkles.

JONTY:

Mandy is helping with make-up and combing the shrimps from his beard.

MISH:

No bad jokes, Jonty. We don't want to upset the most fearsome pirate ever.

JONTY:

You mean like: What's the difference between a hungry pirate and a drunken pirate?

MISH:

Not really appropriate, Jonty.

JONTY:

One rumbles from the tum, the other tumbles from the rum.

MISH:

Moving on... we're now speeding along the coast towards Cape Cod.

JONTY:

Where Captain Bellamy's ghost has already been picked up by jet-ski and is being rushed down to join us and our famous guest.

MISH:

So welcome to our sofa, Captain Blackbeard.

BLACKBEARD:

You'll have to speak up – I've got sand in my ears and a lobster stuck in my vest.

JONTY:

Is your neck alright? Your head looks a bit lopsided.

BLACKBEARD:

You're lucky I've got it on. It's been loose ever since
Maynard chopped it off.

MISH:

Is it true that he threw your headless body into the
sea and you swum three times around your ship
before sinking to the seabed?

BLACKBEARD:

To be honest, I've got no idea. I had other things on
my mind – like a spike.

JONTY:

I have to say, Captain, I was expecting you to be far
more threatening.

BLACKBEARD:

I'm just a puppy really. I used to act like a monster
sometimes just to keep everyone in their place. A fierce
reputation makes the best defence.

MISH:

You must have worked hard on your image; big, hairy,
smart, smoky, grumpy, growly – and just a bit murdery.

BLACKBEARD:

It all worked – and made me rich and successful.

JONTY:

But you didn't live long enough to enjoy it. What happened to all your wealth?

BLACKBEARD:

Ah, so that's why you got me here. I should have known. All you want is my treasure. Well, I'm not telling you. It's safely hidden to stop any thieving pirates from getting their evil hands on it.

MISH:

But you're a pirate yourself.

BLACKBEARD:

Rubbish. Nothing so vulgar. I'm an MTC. That's a Maritime Treasure Collector.

JONTY:

But you delighted in being brutal. You set light to cords in your hair and you twisted your beard around your ears to look like a monster. And they say you drank rum mixed with gunpowder – that's madness!

BLACKBEARD:

It cured my indigestion. One hiccup and my breeches shot out sparks. That's a great party trick to do on deck at night.

MISH:

How did your poor wife cope with all your scary ways?

BLACKBEARD:

Which one?

MISH:

Those wild, staring eyes for a start.

BLACKBEARD:

No, which wife? I think I liked Mary the best.

JONTY:

We're hoping to meet her later. Is it true you had fourteen wives?

BLACKBEARD:

None of your business. Women just seem to fall for my amazing looks.

MISH:

Or maybe it's all that gold you gave them.

BLACKBEARD:

I must have been the richest and most successful of pirates, actually.

VOICE:

Utter rubbish.

JONTY:

Ah ha, I see the ghost of Samuel Bellamy has just arrived on board.

SAMUEL:

(Swaggering on) Well I never, if it isn't my old chum Edward.

BLACKBEARD:

Hey, Sam – I haven't seen you for ages. Not since you drowned at sea at the tender age of 28. At least I lived to be ten years older than you. Like I say, I was by far the more successful, and the richest.

SAMUEL:

Rubbish. I was much richer than you. As soon as you and I left Captain Hornigold, I captured more ships than anyone. I did it by pure skill, without the need to set fire to myself all the time.

BLACKBEARD:

I only did that for show now and again. It made me rich, after all.

SAMUEL:

I had a better head for money. And at least I've still got mine!

BLACKBEARD:

(Drawing sword) Pah – how dare you...

MISH:

Moving on... how about telling us about some of the funny times you had?

SAMUEL:

Ha, like when Edward was first mate on Hornigold's ship? He was always complaining about the rats on the ship. Do you remember?

BLACKBEARD:

I'll never forget. Rats were all over the place. I used to wake up with them crawling inside my hammock and down my nightshirt.

SAMUEL:

They got inside pies in the ship's galley, too. They'd often pop out when you bit into a crust at supper. In fact, I'm thinking of calling my autobiography 'Pie-rats of the Caribbean'.

BLACKBEARD:

That ship's toilet bucket was always heaving with rats. My autobiography is called 'Poo-rats of the Caribbean'. It's already a best seller. Better than yours.

SAMUEL:

(Drawing sword) Pah! How dare you...

MISH:

Moving on... how about telling us about some of the old pirate superstitions?

BLACKBEARD:

There were many of those. Never set sail on a

voyage on a Friday, otherwise it's doomed. That's where you must have gone wrong, Sam. Either that or you whistled on deck. Whistling on a boat is said to conjure up a storm.

SAMUEL:

At least I never ate a banana on board ship. That's said to cause bad luck.

JONTY:

But it could stop you dying from scurvy. *(They stare.)* Just saying.

MISH:

You didn't know then that the disease scurvy was caused by a poor diet with no fruit and vegetables.

BLACKBEARD:

That explains a lot.

JONTY:

How did you forecast the weather on your ship?

SAMUEL:

Easy. I just hung up seaweed in the rigging.

MISH:

How did that work?

SAMUEL:

If it's wet, it must be raining. If it's dry, it's going to rain soon.

BLACKBEARD:

Red sky at night – 'tis a pirate's delight...

SAMUEL:

Red sky at noon – we're on fire, yer buffoon!
(They both roar with laughter.)

MISH:

I'm glad to see you're both getting on so well.

SAMUEL:

I suppose Ed ain't so bad. I've never seen him with such a massive beard.

JONTY:

Maybe he had to line up too long for a shave from the ship's barber. After all, in summer there's nothing like a good barber-queue on board ship!

MISH:

We said 'no jokes', Jonty.

JONTY:

(In a pirate voice.) Or did you use the baaaaarrrber at the haaaaarrrrbour?

BLACKBEARD:

Are you trying to be funny?

MISH:

Er... moving on

SAMUEL:

(Roaring with laughter.) Baaaaarrrber at the haaaaarrrrbour – that's hilaaaarrrious!

BLACKBEARD:

Yeah – it's enough to make me laurrrrrgh my head off! *(They both guffaw.)*

JONTY:

On that bombshell, we'd better move on to the rest of the story.

MISH:

Please stay with us, captains, for a more relaxed chat with some other ghosts shortly. In the meantime, we return to the giant plasma screen to see how pirates liked to punish anyone who upset them...

Pirate punishments

PIRATE CAPTAINS HAVE MANY WAYS TO PUNISH SOMEONE WHO ANNOYS THEM...

BUT I HATE COCONUTS!

MAROONING.

WHIPPING WITH A CAT O'NINE TAILS.

JUST WAIT TILL WE RUB SALT AND VINEGAR IN YOUR WOUNDS.

BILBOES: GETTING LOCKED IN WRIST AND LEG IRONS.

PLEASE HELP, I'VE GOT AN ITCH!

THERE'S NOTHING WORSE THAN BARNACLES ON THE BOTTOM.

KEELHAULING: BEING SCRAPED UNDER THE SHIP AGAINST ITS SHARP BARNACLES.

HOW CAN YOU REFUSE TO TALK?

TORTURE: TO MAKE A PRISONER TALK.

Ghosts reunited

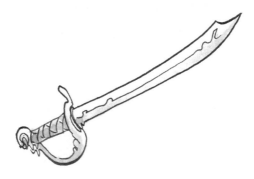

MISH:

Welcome back to the *Live from the Crypt* sofa, where we're delighted to have the ghosts of Captain Blackbeard and Samuel Bellamy still with us and about to meet another mystery ghost who hopes to join us.

JONTY:

Yes, this is 'Ghosts reunited' where we bring together ghosts who haven't met for a while, which could make for an interesting encounter. We are hoping to link up with our guests' old boss, Captain Benjamin Hornigold, another pirate who drowned at sea.

HORNIGOLD:

An occupational hazard. My ship was wrecked on a reef during the 1719 hurricane season off the Bahamas. Most annoying. I was the third of us three to perish in three years. Bad luck, I reckon.

BELLAMY:

Or a bad captain. We left you because we could do better on our own.

BLACKBEARD:

You refused to attack any British ship, but we believed in attacking anyone.

BELLAMY:

So what happened to you, Hornigold?

BLACKBEARD:

Pah! The last I heard, he sailed to Jamaica with the *Ranger* in January 1718 and received a pardon from the governor there if he gave up pirating.

HORNIGOLD:

That's right, and what's more, I became a pirate hunter for the governor of the Bahamas.

BELLAMY:

You traitor.

BLACKBEARD:

What a turncoat. I bet it was you who told the navy where I was hiding. Officer Maynard was the one who got me in the end.

JONTY:

And you might like to know that even today, his naval unit still celebrates Blackbeard Night at an annual dinner to mark 22nd November.

MISH:

And the city of Hampton in Virginia holds an annual Blackbeard Festival where they recreate your final sea battle on tall ships in the harbour.

BLACKBEARD:

That's disgraceful.

HORNIGOLD:

You should have seen all the celebrations when you were killed, Edward. Everyone was pleased to see the back of you.

BELLAMY:

At least we were killed by the mighty ocean rather than a sailor on a boat.

BLACKBEARD:

I find that very hurtful. Even savage pirates have feelings, you know.

MISH:

Talking of feelings, your wife has just joined us from Bath.

JONTY:

I hope she's dressed.

MISH:

From Bath, North Carolina. Live by satellite.

BLACKBEARD:

Fancy seeing you, dear.

MARY:

Nice to see you BB.

HORNIGOLD:

He had thirteen wives before you, you know.

BELLAMY:

Whatever did you see in this big, ugly, hairy, aggressive millionaire?

MARY:

He was nice to me and I quite like gold. I was only sixteen.

MISH:

What was your wedding like?

BLACKBEARD:

Plenty of rum.

MARY:

We married in 1718 and the ceremony was conducted by Governor Charles Eden. My father wasn't too happy – he was William Ormand, a plantation owner, and it was our plan to settle down and run a plantation ourselves.

BLACKBEARD:

Yeah, but I got restless. The sea kept calling.

MARY:

So did I, sweetheart.

BLACKBEARD:

Yeah, but not as loud as the sea. Piracy was in my blood, so off I went once more.

MARY:

Leaving me all on my own *(sobs)*. He never returned. They caught him just months later. I was so upset – I wouldn't get any more treasure. That hurt.

BLACKBEARD:

Not as much as it hurt me. My neck has never been the same since.

MARY:

I should have married that nice Welsh pirate called Bartholomew Roberts. He was a proper gentleman and captured far more ships that you lot put together. And being Welsh, he'd have sung to me each day... until his throat went.

JONTY:

I must interrupt you there, Mary, before you upset Blackbeard further, make him turn nasty or tell us about Bartholomew Roberts. His story is coming up next on our plasma storyboard. Stay tuned for this piratey comic strip...

OVER TO A COTTAGE IN WALES...

Bartholomew Roberts gets it in the neck

BABY ROBERTS IS BORN IN WALES IN 1682.

YOU'D MAKE A GREAT WELSH RUGBY PLAYER IF YOU WERE BORN 150 YEARS LATER.

I'D BETTER BE A PIRATE, THEN.

HAVE YOU HEARD THEY'VE JUST KILLED BLACKBEARD?

HMM, THAT MEANS THERE'S A VACANCY.

BARTHOLOMEW ROBERTS JOINS THE NAVY BEFORE SAILING ON A SLAVE SHIP IN 1718.

1720: ROBERTS LEADS A FLEET OF PIRATE SHIPS IN THE CARIBBEAN.

I MUST BE THE RICHEST PIRATE EVER.

IN HIS 4 YEARS AS A PIRATE, ROBERTS CAPTURES OVER 400 SHIPS.

1722: PIRATE HUNTERS ATTACK OFF THE COAST OF AFRICA.

I DON'T LIKE TO SHOW OFF, BUT I'VE GOT 500 PIRATES UNDER MY COMMAND. SO MUCH FOR BLACKBEARD!

OUCH, I'VE BEEN SHOT IN THE NECK!

BARTHOLOMEW ROBERTS IS KILLED AND OVER 150 OF HIS PIRATES ARE ARRESTED AND SENT TO TRIAL. IT IS THE END OF AN ERA.

119

Spin the news

ALEEMA:

And now it's 'Spin the news' where I spin a dial for the news headlines from a mystery year *(spins a dial which stops at 1701)*. 1701. It was the year of a big news story that echoed around Britain and America. On screen to tell us about it is the ghost of Captain Kidd, coming to us from his final resting place at the bottom of the River Thames near Tilbury Point.

KIDD:

How do you do?

ALEEMA:

It's good to have you with us, Captain Kidd. Before we talk about 1701, can I ask about the years before then?

KIDD:

Aye, you can. I was born in Dundee, Scotland and began sailing when I was a wee lad. I don't want to talk about 1701, particularly May 23rd. I should never have been hanged for piracy. It was all a big stitch-up.

ALEEMA:

Well, there's no doubt you were a privateer in the 1690s and you attacked French ships for the English government.

KIDD:

I was also hired to rid the sea of pirates and capture their ships. Admittedly I clung on to some of their loot, just to keep it from falling into the wrong hands.

ALEEMA:

Today you're known as the pirate with buried treasure.

KIDD:

Aye, and I'm not telling you where it is, either.

ALEEMA:

You're also known as being the unluckiest pirate ever to sail the high seas. Just as you started out as a privateer, the law changed and made you an outlaw.

KIDD:

Exactly. One minute I was working as a pirate hunter for the East India Company and the next minute I was being hunted as a ruthless criminal.

ALEEMA:

What did your wife have to say about that?

KIDD:

Quite a lot. Sarah had a lot to say about most things.

ALEEMA:

That's good, because she is joining us on screen from New York. Welcome to 'Spin the news', Sarah Rousby.

SARAH:

William, it's good to see you.

KIDD:

Where did the name Rousby come from?

SARAH:

I remarried. You were my third husband and after 1701 I married my fourth, seeing as you had gone. If you remember, I got arrested as well as you. After our eight years of marriage, I was hunted down as well and locked up in New York.

KIDD:

I heard about that – whilst they shipped me back to England to go on trial. They found me guilty of piracy and murder, just because I collected some treasure and hit one of my crew over the head with a big bucket.

ALEEMA:

He must have gone a little pail! I guess getting rid of him was on your bucket list. See what I did there?

KIDD:

It broke his skull. I didn't mean to kill him. They sentenced me to hang.

SARAH:

Poor William. I couldn't even hold your hand in your last hours. Never mind, they released me from prison, gave me back our stuff and I found a new husband. He thought I knew where you'd buried your treasure, but I didn't.

KIDD:

I was thinking of you when they led me at low tide to Execution Dock at Wapping. The huge crowds shouted and jeered and I shouted back. I stood beneath the gallows as the noose went round my neck... but I fell to the ground. The rope snapped and I landed splat in the mud. I told them it meant I must be innocent but they wouldn't listen.

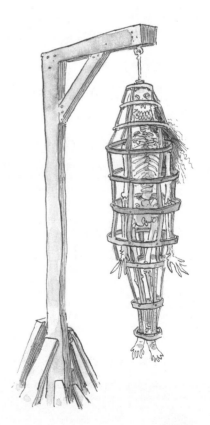

SARAH:

Poor William. That's so sad. But tell me, where is your treasure now?

KIDD:

That's the secret I took with me as they hoisted me up again. My dead body was taken to be hanged in chains at Tilbury Point for the world to see, as an example to all pirates. It was very degrading.

SARAH:

Poor William. You may like to know that with what wealth you left me I bought a tavern in New York, which I ran till I died in 1744. Mind you, I never told customers I'd been the wife of the infamous Captain Kidd.

ALEEMA:

They'd have thought you were just kidding. See what I did there?

KIDD:

I'm not staying around for any more of this nonsense. Besides, the tide is coming in and I'm stuck in the mud.

SARAH:

Poor William. It's been nice to hang around with you again. Oops, I didn't mean to say that. Sorry.

ALEEMA:

On that note, we had better end this edition of 'Spin the news'. Viewers might be interested to know that 1701 was also the year when the French began building a settlement in America – now the city of Detroit. That same year, Yale University was founded in Connecticut. So 1701 wasn't all bad.

KIDD:

I beg to differ.

SARAH:

Poor William. Now, about that treasure...

ALEEMA:

We must leave it there. William and Sarah Kidd certainly made the news headlines in 1701. Thank you for joining us. There's just time to leap forward 100 years to another part of the world where pirate action was causing a stir. Let's return to the giant plasma screen storyboard to meet the scariest woman pirate of them all...

Ching Shih
and the Red Flag fleet

1801: THE CHINA SEA IS TERRORISED BY HUNDREDS OF JUNKS AND THOUSANDS OF PIRATES OF THE RED FLAG FLEET.

BOATS AND HOMES ALONG THE CHINESE COAST ARE ROBBED AND PLUNDERED DURING 10 YEARS OF TERROR.

CAPTAIN CHING SHIH RULES THE PIRATE FLEET WITH RUTHLESS CRUELTY.

I KILL ANYONE WHO GETS IN MY WAY – AND ANYONE WHO DOESN'T.

YAY – I PUT THE 'CHING' INTO KER-CHING!

GREAT, I LOVE A GOOD PUNCH-UP.

1808: THE CHINESE NAVY SETS SAIL TO ATTACK CHING SHIH'S FLEET.

Sink or Swim
(A pirate game to find pirate 'pieces of fake')

GAIL:

Welcome to 'Sink or swim', the gameshow where ghosts tell us their pirate tales. Each team member will try to smuggle a lie past the opposing team. If the false fact is correctly spotted by the opposite team, they win a point – but if it isn't, the first team wins the point. It's not so much about 'pieces of eight' as 'pieces of fake'. Let's meet the teams...

RACHEL:

Hello, I'm Rachel Wall, the captain of the Sinkers Team. We're three pirates who didn't last long and met grim ends. We may have been unlucky sinkers in life but we're going to be lucky tonight. By the way, unlike my fellow pirates here, I'm American born, bred and dead. I am joined by two pirates who knew each other well: Mary Read and Jack Rackham, also known as Calico Jack.

LADY K:

Hello, I'm Mary Wolverston, also known as Lady Killigrew. I'm the captain of the Swimmers Team – three pirates who managed to survive longer than most. I'm English, whilst my colleagues are Irish and Welsh: Anne Bonny and Henry Morgan. We hope to swim away from the game with plenty of points tonight.

GAIL:

So now we've met the teams, I shall ask Rachel to start by telling us her pirate tale, then Lady Killigrew will chat with her team and decide which of Rachel's details is fake and must be sunk forever. So it's over to you, Rachel.

RACHEL:

Sure thing. These are my details but one of them is false. My name was Rachel Schmidt and when I was 16, I was attacked by a gang of girls at the harbour. A guy called George Wall came to my rescue and hey-ho we soon got married! We joined a bunch of sailors and before we knew it we were living on a ramshackle ship. Then came our stroke of genius. After bad weather in 1781, we made it look like we were sinking and I called for help to a passing ship. As soon as it docked alongside, we stormed aboard and robbed it. What easy money, even if a few sailors got killed. We carried on like that but after a few years I got caught. I admitted to being a pirate but denied ever killing anyone. Even so, they hanged me in 1789 when I was 29. I was the first American woman to become a pirate and the last woman to be hanged in Massachusetts, where you can admire a bronze life-size statue of me today.

GAIL:

Thank you for your story, Rachel. But which of those details is made up? That's for Lady Killigrew and her team to guess. I can see they are busily arguing among themselves, so what have you decided?

LADY K:

It all sounds reasonable to me but my team thinks it's all rubbish! We know you were hanged but did you really do those things? Surely pirates are swashbuckling athletes who swing onto ships, have a good fight and take away valuable cargo. Would you be so mean as to plead for help, lure sailors on board and then attack them? You don't look that mean, so I'm going to say that bit was a lie.

GAIL:

Well, let's see. Rachel, were you really so mean that you attacked sailors who were kind enough to come to your rescue?

RACHEL:

It was... TRUE. That's exactly what we did!

GAIL:

So what was the fib you smuggled into your story?

RACHEL:

The very last bit. There has never been a life-size statue of me anywhere. Yet!

GAIL:

Never say never. Maybe after this programme, they'll think about it. So that's a point to the Sinkers Team. Can we have Lady Killigrew's story for the Swimmers to sort the fact from the fiction?

LADY K:

I lived during the reign of Queen Elizabeth in England. Her majesty encouraged my father to be a gentleman pirate by robbing Spanish ships. My husband, Lord John Killigrew, did the same. I sometimes sailed with him from our castle in Cornwall and robbed any ship that happened to be passing. In 1583, a Spanish treasure ship docked near our castle so I invited its captain and crew to stay with us. One night, as they slept, I led a raid and seized the ship's cargo. It was great fun, but I was accused of piracy. My son was the local judge so he managed to get me off. Unfortunately,

some of the treasure was found in my home so I was put on trial and sentenced to death. Just before I was to be executed, Queen Elizabeth sent word to let me off. I think my son's bribes may have helped. But I got away with it and was even invited to a royal banquet with her majesty and given a necklace.

GAIL:

Thank you, Lady Killigrew. It seems you were an upper-class pirate with style who lived before everyone else here – unless you made up the date. So it's now back to Rachel and her team. They are already discussing amongst themselves. So what was the pirate piffle and Cornish codswallop?

RACHEL:

We think it's all that castle stuff. Anyone living in a grand castle by the sea wouldn't need to go pirating. We think Lady Killigrew didn't live in a castle and probably wasn't even very wealthy.

GAIL:

In that case, we will return to Lady Killigrew to ask if living in a Cornish castle was fantasy or fact. Do tell us.

LADY K:

It was... TRUE. We lived at Pendennis Castle. My story was all true apart from the last part. Queen Elizabeth did not invite me to a banquet to give me a necklace. She did, however, stop me from being executed.

GAIL:

In that case, each team now has one point, so let's see if The Sinkers can manage to score again as we ask Mary Read to tell us her story.

MARY:

Right, I'll get right to the point as I'm known for being very blunt, unlike my sword. Although I dressed as a man, I got married on ship and, when my new husband got in a fight, I took over. He was about to have a duel with another pirate but as I was better at fighting, I said I'd take his place. So I finished off the pirate with just one karate chop on the neck and kept my husband! Then I was arrested with Jack Rackham and Anne Bonny in 1720 and went on trial in Jamaica. By then I was expecting a baby and I pleaded to be allowed to live and lead an honest life with my child. They agreed but I caught a fever in prison and I died the following year so I'm a very disappointed ghost!

GAIL:

Sadly, it didn't end well for you, Mary – but your career choice had a lot to do with it. But which little snippet was pure pirate poppycock? It's now over to Lady Killigrew and her team to sift the flotsam from the jetsam...

LADY K:

Now this is tricky, because my team member knew Mary well and thinks it's all true, even the date and little details. We know you had fights with pirates, but we're not sure about that karate chop – whatever that is! Anne says you would have used a pistol, so we think that bit was a lie.

GAIL:

So was it, Mary? Was your killer punch to the neck true or false?

MARY:

It was... FALSE. Anne knows me too well; I fought with pistols and daggers but was much better than any man. I was a stronger fighter than my husband – not that it did me any good in the end.

GAIL:

So at the end of that story, The Sinkers have one point and The Swimmers have two. Let's see how the score changes with Henry Morgan's story next.

HENRY:

Although I say it myself, I was a dashing Welsh pirate captain who got very rich and enjoyed a comfortable retirement. In 1669 I led 8 ships and 650 sailors to attack anything Spanish, then raided the city of Panama. After conquering the fort, my army hacked through the jungle, defeated Spanish forces and raided the city, burning it to the ground. We tortured many to find where all the treasures were kept. All good fun, but I got arrested for my ruthless deeds. King Charles II gave me a pardon for upsetting the Spanish, knighted me and gave me the nice job of looking after sunny Jamaica as Governor. As I'd buried a lot of gold in Montego Bay, I just had to pop out with a spade if cash ran low or I needed to buy more rum. Not that I had to, as I owned sugar plantations and many slaves. I died in 1688, aged 53 – not bad for a dashing Welsh pirate scoundrel!

GAIL:

You sound quite a character, Henry – or should I call you Sir Henry? Who can tell if you were lying or telling the truth? Over to you, Rachel.

RACHEL:

Hmm, we've all heard of you and we know you got very rich, but we just can't decide which of those details was baloney. I can't think you'd have been knighted by the King of England for being a pirate, but my team says there's no way you'd bury gold on the beach and risk it being found. So, I say your buried treasure in Montego Bay is a lie.

GAIL:

Let's ask Henry. Was buried treasure a buried lie? Was your hidden gold true?

HENRY:

It was... FALSE. I spent my fortune rather than bury it.

GAIL:

So you guessed right, Rachel. Your team now has another point. Can Jack Rackham score you one more, I wonder? Over to you, Calico Jack.

JACK:

I commanded a pirate ship called the *Ranger* and they called me Calico Jack after the expensive silk fabric I wore, stitched with my own design of a skull and crossbones on the back. Most of my raids were around the Caribbean, with my wife Anne Bonny and our good friend Mary Read. We got up to adventures till October 1720, when our luck ran out. Pirate-hunter Jonathan Barnet tracked us down to a bay in Jamaica and surprised us while we were partying after a raid. He captured us and sentenced us all to hang. On 18th November they took me to Gallows Point in Port Royal where I was publicly executed. My body was later taken down and displayed in chains, swinging from a gibbet – my beautiful calico shirt pecked to bits by birds. Tragic.

GAIL:

So what do The Swimmers make of that tale? I'm sure Anne Bonny must know all of that so it should be easy to spot the fib, so what is it?

LADY K:

If only we knew! It all seems so likely to me and Anne wonders if it's the date that's wrong. She thinks you were hanged closer to your birthday on 16th December... so we'll say 18th November 1720 was not your execution date.

GAIL:

Over to you, Jack Rackham. Was that dreaded date true or false?

JACK:

It was... TRUE. How could my own wife forget the dreaded day? I can't believe she didn't remember my shirts! They weren't silk at all. Calico is a type of rustic cotton and, even though I was credited for the Jolly Roger design, I didn't wear it on my back. That would make me an ideal target for a pistol shot!

GAIL:

In that case, The Sinkers score another point. Can the Swimmers score next to end the game in a tie? Over to Anne Bonny for our final story tonight.

ANNE:

It just goes to show I never bothered to notice what Jack wore! I was born and grew up in Ireland and married a sailor called John Bonny. But that was all rather dull and a more exciting life on Calico Jack Rackham's ship got me into the pirate world. I dressed as a man and killed anyone who suspected I was a woman. Along with Jack, Mary Read and our crew, we sailed the Caribbean as robbers until our arrest. Like Mary, I was expecting a baby so I couldn't be executed. I gave birth in prison and was released. I went back to Ireland, took back my old name of Anne Cormac, became a nun and died an old lady in 1782.

GAIL:

What could possibly be a fake fact in all of that? It's up to Rachel to decide...

RACHEL:

Well, Jack and Mary tell me it's all true apart from maybe the last bit. They don't think you'd ever be let out of prison, as women were executed soon after they'd had their baby. So, we say you died not long after Jack and Mary.

GAIL:

You certainly seem to be sure and united, so we'll ask Anne to tell us if her release from prison really did happen. True or false?

ANNE:

It was... TRUE. They let me out eventually and I didn't return to piracy but lived to a ripe old age. Of course, I missed you all and the bit I made up was going back to my old name and becoming a nun. That just didn't happen!

GAIL:

Well, that's certainly a fascinating thought to finish on, with the final score a tie. Thank you to both teams, for telling us your own true stories with a few whopping lies thrown in. We have managed to feed the fibs to the sharks to sink forever and let the truth swim to the surface and sail off into the sunset. So that's all from us here, as I hand you back to Mish and Jonty on the studio sofa. Good night.

For the wreck-ord

MISH:

You join us back on the *Live from the Crypt* sofa where our two ghostly guests have been listening to everything with great interest.

JONTY:

Yes, maybe Blackbeard or Sam Bellamy would like to tell us any thoughts about the pirates and wrecks we've heard about – purely for the wreck-ord!

151

BLACKBEARD:

Going back to Captain Kidd, I didn't know him but we heard all about him. He sailed to Madagascar off east Africa and turned the island into his stronghold where he kept his ship, the *Adventure Galley.* That was a 300-ton ship with 34 cannons. I decided to have even more on my ship.

MISH:

In fact, Madagascar was once swarming with pirates and there's a big pirate cemetery there. The island of Sainte-Marie off east Madagascar is full of the bones of pirates who terrorised the seas during the 17th and 18th centuries.

JONTY:

And we've spoken to many of the ghosts there for this programme. About 1,000 pirates lived there and it's now a thriving tourist area. I visited the crumbling graves now covered by swaying grass – spookily peaceful, despite the bones of violent killers. That's why I didn't go after dark, but went nightclubbing instead.

BELLAMY:

I'll tell you about a pirate you haven't mentioned. Henry Every was amazing. His ship *Fancy* had 46 guns and was one of the fastest ships around. He got so rich he retired and never got arrested or killed in a battle or a wreck. Some say he lived in luxury as a self-made king on Madagascar, with thousands of his crew as servants. Now that's what I call success!

BLACKBEARD:

I reckon I was just as successful, apart from getting my head chopped off.

MISH:

Talking of which, we've just had a text from Mary Critchett of Virginia, who was hanged for piracy there in 1729. She says: 'Never mind about Blackbeard's head, don't you know about the pirate Nicholas Brown? Look him up.'

JONTY:

Which is what our producer has just done and it says: 'Nicholas Brown was killed in battle by pirate hunter and former schoolmate John Drudge in 1726.

Brown's head was cut off and pickled in rum as proof, so that Drudge could collect the reward of £500 offered by the Jamaican government.'

BELLAMY:

The moral of that story is: always beware of your school friends!

JONTY:

Or you might end up in a rather rum situation. See what I did there?

MISH:

Moving on... we've really enjoyed having you both on our *Live from the Crypt* sofa and would love to talk more – so how about another reunion sometime?

JONTY:

How about if we all meet up for Blackbeard's 350th birthday around 2030 for a party at the pirate cemetery on the Île Sainte-Marie of Madagascar?

MISH:

That would be awesome. You two could meet up with ghostly pirate friends for plenty of spooky swashbuckling and to re-live old times.

JONTY:

Great idea, Mish. Maybe I'll give that one a miss and stay in the nightclub. Let's wreck-omend to all our reckless pirate ghosts to join us.

BELLAMY:

(Standing aggressively.) Will you stop going on about wrecks? I've had enough. It's about time you were keelhauled for your smug and stupid jokes...

BLACKBEARD:

(Waving a pistol.) I agree, my old friend. This chatty landlubber must be challenged to a duel. Let's see how he likes losing his head...

MISH:

Moving on... Whilst Jonty runs from our sofa and jumps overboard, it just remains for me to say a big thank you to all our ghost guests, even those who are about to turn nasty. So it's goodnight from Jonty Yardley somewhere in the ocean and from me, Mish Varma...

ALL:

(shouting/sneering/growling) Good night.

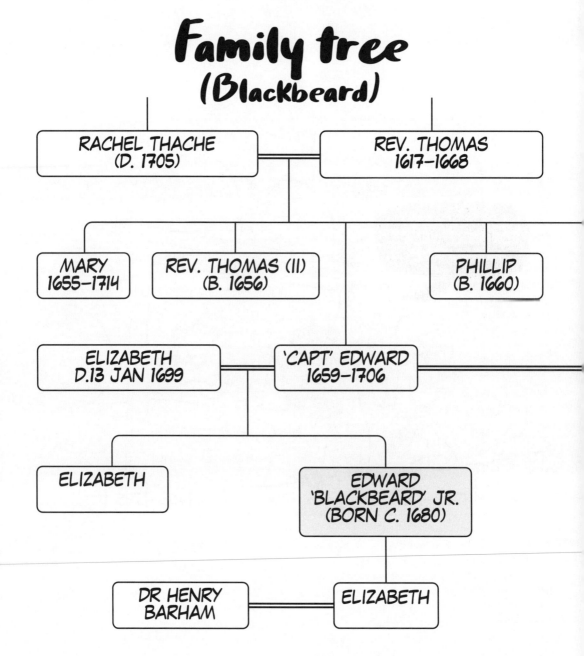

Family tree
(Blackbeard)

| RACHEL THACHE (D. 1705) | REV. THOMAS 1617–1668 |

MARY 1655–1714

REV. THOMAS (II) (B. 1656)

PHILLIP (B. 1660)

ELIZABETH D.13 JAN 1699

'CAPT' EDWARD 1659–1706

ELIZABETH

EDWARD 'BLACKBEARD' JR. (BORN C. 1680)

DR HENRY BARHAM

ELIZABETH

Interviews with the Ghosts of PIRATES

```
┌─────────────┬─────────────┬─────────────┬─────────────┐
│  ABIGAIL    │   ROBERT    │  SUSANNAH   │   RACHEL    │
│  (B. 1663)  │  (B. 1664)  │    SELF     │  PHILLIPS   │
└─────────────┴─────────────┴─────────────┴─────────────┘

        ┌──────────────────────────────────────┐
        │  LUCRETIA (POQUET MAVERLY) AXTELL     │
        └──────────────────────────────────────┘

        ┌─────────────┬─────────────┬─────────────┐
        │    COX      │   RACHEL    │   THOMAS    │
        │  1700–1737  │  (B. 1704)  │  1705–1748  │
        └─────────────┴─────────────┴─────────────┘
```

Pirate timeline

700–100 BC

Pirates are reported around Ancient Greece, then Ancient Rome.

200 AD

Piracy increases in Asia after the fall of the Chinese Han dynasty.

700–1000

Vikings from northern Europe make raids along coastal areas in North America, Europe and North Africa.

1300s

Piracy rises around the Mediterranean. English and French fleets join forces in battles against African-based corsairs.

1401

Klaus Störtebeker, one of the most famous German pirates, is beheaded.

1500s

A rise in ocean trade traffic brings a big increase in piracy. Ships and towns are attacked in newly-discovered America.

1550s/60s

Conflict between England and Spain sees the rise of privateers, such as Sir Francis Drake and Lady Killigrew.

1623–1638

The Caribbean becomes a haven for pirates. Over 500 ships are robbed in 15 years.

1650–1680

Britain and France attack Spanish shipping lanes and ports, beginning the 'Golden Age of Piracy'.

1690s

Caribbean-based pirates sail in search of trade ships travelling to and from India. Pirate Captain Henry Every captures an Indian treasure ship full of riches – one of the biggest pirate hoards ever.

1701

Scottish pirate William Kidd is executed in London.

1717

Samuel Bellamy and most of his crew aboard the *Whydah* perish in a hurricane off the coast of Cape Cod when his treasure-laden ship capsizes.

1718

Blackbeard is killed in battle with Robert Maynard of the British Navy.

1720

Captain Jack Rackham and his two female shipmates, Anne Bonny and Mary Read, are captured. Rackham is hanged.

1722

Welshman Bartholomew Roberts (one of the wealthiest pirates) is killed in battle.

1716–1730

The final stage of the 'Golden Age of Piracy'. Although European countries cease fighting each other, many ex-privateers refuse to stop robbing ships. The navies of Europe and America hunt them down.

1775–1800
Piracy returns to the Atlantic and Mediterranean during the American Revolution and Napoleonic Wars.

EARLY 1800S
Pirate captain Ching Shih leads thousands of Asian pirates on the China Sea.

1820S
Policing oceans halts piracy around Central America and eventually in Asia.

2000S
A rise in pirate activity around Somalia on the East African coast.

Quiz –
Who wants to be a privateer?

Who Wants to be a Privateer (with a chance to win a
million pieces of eight)?

(You can play this quiz on your own or with a contestant,
a question-host and an audience.)

1. For 100 – Part of the 17th & 18th centuries is sometimes called the golden 'what' of piracy?
a) Ticket
b) Ship
c) Pants
d) Age

2. For 200 – Where was one of the main hunting areas for pirates?
a) Sherwood Forest
b) The Great Barrier Reef
c) The Caribbean
d) New York

3. For 300 – Which of these was a well-known pirate?
a) Blackbeard
b) Black Eyebrows
c) Greenbeard
d) Purple Knickers

4. For 500 – Which of these was a real Scottish pirate?
a) Hamish Swashbuckle
b) Captain Kidd
c) Captain Kipper
d) Edward McBeardface

5. For 1,000 – Where is the wreck of Samuel Bellamy's pirate ship the *Whydah*?
a) Bermuda
b) Florida
c) Cape Cod
d) Montego Bay

6. For 2,000 – What was the name of Edward Thache's ship?
a) Queen Mary's Behind
b) Queen Anne's Revenge
c) Queen Anne's Rampage
d) Queen Elizabeth's Revolt

7. For 4,000 – Which pirate was known as the Robin Hood of the Sea?
a) Benjamin Hornigold
b) James Rackham
c) Samuel Bellamy
d) Bartholomew Roberts

8. For 8,000 – By the 1570s, which 2 countries were often attacking each other's ships?
a) England and Spain
b) America and Jamaica
c) France and China
d) Scotland and Germany

9. For 16,000 – In 1715 many Spanish treasure ships were wrecked in a hurricane off which coast?
a) Bermuda
b) Florida
c) Cuba
d) California

10. For 32,000 – Who was Robert Maynard?
a) An Irish pirate
b) The Governor of Jamaica
c) A Navy Officer
d) The hangman of the Caribbean

11. For 64,000 – When were Mary Read and Anne Bonny captured?
a) 1717
b) 1718
c) 1719
d) 1720

12. For 125,000 – What were Buccaneers?
a) Privateers of the Caribbean
b) Corsairs of the Mediterranean
c) Pirates of Madagascar
d) Bandits in the China Sea

13. For 250,000 – What did pirates call the bottom of the ocean?
a) The final hammock
b) Dead man's rest
c) Davy Jones's locker
d) Long John's trunk

14. For 500,000 – Getting dragged under a ship on a rope as a punishment was called what?
a) Hornswaggling
b) Barnacle-scraping
c) Shark-baiting
d) Keelhauling

15. For 1 million – Which pirate had his head pickled in rum?
a) John Drudge
b) Henry Every
c) Klaus Störtebeker
d) Nicholas Brown

The points you win entitle you to a treasure map to help you find your prize, which includes the action movie based on this book (a pirate copy, of course!).

ANSWERS:
1 (D) 2 (C) 3 (A) 4 (B) 5 (C)
6 (B) 7 (C) 8 (A) 9 (B) 10 (C) 11 (D)
12 (A) 13 (C) 14 (D) 15 (D)

Glossary

BILBOES
Iron shackles (like handcuffs for ankles) used to fetter prisoners' feet.

FLOTSAM
Floating wreckage and cargo of a ship that has sunk.

GALLEON
A large three-masted sailing ship used by the Spaniards from the 15th to 17th centuries.

GIBBET
A gallows to execute criminals by hanging and for the public exhibition of those hanged.

JETSAM
Objects thrown from a ship, often washed up on the shore.

PRIVATEER
A sailor on a privately owned armed ship hired by a country to attack or capture enemy ships.

RANSOM
Payment demanded in return for setting a kidnapped person free.

SCURVY
Disease caused by not having enough vitamin C in the diet, leading to severe weakness and bleeding gums.

SLOOP
A sailing boat with one mast and sails that reach from one end of the boat to the other.

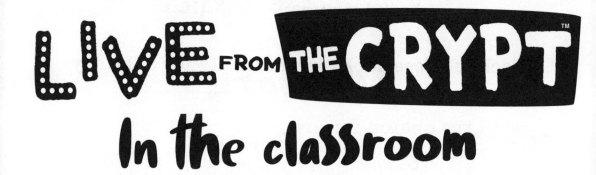

In the classroom

10 Titles in chronological order:

Tutankhamun
Ancient Egypt and Howard Carter's 1922 discoveries.

Qin Shi Huang
Ancient China and the Terracotta Army discovery of 1974.

Roman Emperors
Ancient Rome and the first 5 notorious emperors after Julius Caesar.

Henry VIII
Tudor England and the turbulent trials of king and country.

Pirates
17th & 18th century swashbuckling on the high seas and the Caribbean.

Queen Victoria
The life and times of an enigmatic queen and her Victorian world.

Louis Pasteur
The age of scientific discovery: disease, germ theory and hygiene.

Sparky Inventors
The age of electricity pioneers; from Thomas Edison to Nikola Tesla.

Women Doctors and Medical Pioneers
Marie Curie and the first women Nobel prize-winners.

Titanic
The famous tragedy told by those who were there.

(Arranging the books in order could be an activity in itself!)

Each of these books is primarily for solitary reading, but they have also been designed with the option for groups to read and perform together as a play at school, home or anywhere else.

A whole class can be included, or smaller groups if individuals take on several parts. There are plenty of flexible possibilities to involve as many or as few as required.

The books can be broken up into their various scenes for reading, performing or recording on video or audio equipment separately, simultaneously or with everyone together. On the other hand, one solitary individual could, with different voices, record scenes alone. The ultimate aim is that all who read or perform should be entertained, informed, engaged and encouraged to enjoy plenty of imaginative factual fun.

Ideas for performance

As well as the 20 or so character parts in each book, there is plenty of scope for extra roles for both performers and creators behind the scenes.

Potential extra roles

FACT-CHECKER(S)

Throughout the script, various bizarre facts with unusual information appear. Occasionally a flag/banner could pop up saying 'That's TRUE!' (Maybe with an added comment such as 'Yes, they really did eat x'.) Someone could verify such facts or add an extra detail, then be responsible for holding up the sign at the appropriate time in the show.

CONTESTANTS

A few willing volunteers to sit the final quiz could swot up on information before sitting in the hotseat. If a contestant chooses the wrong answer, a replacement volunteer can take over from where they left off. Four lifelines are available: 50-50 (2 wrong answers removed), ask the host, ask the audience and ask a friend.

DIRECTOR

A suitable person will need to take control of fitting everything together, making decisions and directing the cast (as well as taking the blame!)

SOUND EFFECTS

Someone could be responsible for recording/playing appropriate sound effects, TV jingles and songs/music between scenes or to link sections. Anyone so inspired and skilled could adapt the comic strip sequences for PowerPoint (or some such) visual presentation for showing on screen.

QUIZ HOST

The questioner can read out each question followed by the four possible answers, or a PowerPoint slide can be prepared for showing each question. A second slide can also be prepared with two wrong answers omitted, should the contestant ask for the 50-50 option. The questioner shouldn't see the answer until the contestant says 'final answer', particularly if the 'ask the host' lifeline has been chosen. If the 'ask the audience' lifeline is chosen, the host asks everyone to vote for each answer in turn by raising a hand (voting only once!). After counting the votes for each question, the host repeats the figures to the contestant. If the 'ask a friend' lifeline is used, the contestant will already have chosen someone in the audience to ask. The host invites the friend to give an answer, checks if they are correct and announces the result.

Additional activities

CHARACTER CARDS

All the characters in the book (whether a genuine historical character or from the TV team) can be summarised on a card with simple headings, scores and personality characteristics. These can then be discussed, displayed or even 'played' if players compare their cards or devise 'Top Trump'-style activities. Lists of character traits/adjectives can be added, with students having to justify why they have chosen their descriptions. Some examples follow:

CHARACTER CARD	
NAME:	

DATES:	COUNTRY:

STRENGTH	
WEAKNESS	
SKILL	
BIG MOMENT	
QUOTE	

CALM	SILLY	GRUMPY	ANGRY
CHALLENGING	CHEERFUL	POMPOUS	CLUMSY
CONFIDENT	MISERABLE	TENSE	DULL
GOOD-NATURED	CAPABLE	NERVOUS	LAZY
WISE	CHARMING	SELFISH	SHY
DREAMY	ENTHUSIASTIC	CARING	SCARY
STUBBORN	KIND	CLEVER	LIVELY
ANXIOUS	WITTY	FRIENDLY	PATIENT
CRUEL	INTENSE	SENSITIVE	SLEEPY
GLOOMY	TOUGH	ARGUMENTATIVE	GIGGLY
MOODY	DOMINEERING	SARCASTIC	BORED

TIMELINE TEASER

This could be a puzzle for individuals/pairs or a timed group competition. It would feature the timeline at the back of the book. A photocopy with a few blanks, together with a choice of answers displayed elsewhere, should keep everyone happily amused, engaged and even enraged! This offers a great way of consolidating understanding of the context of the events in the book.

MATCH THE MEANING

Chopping up a copy of the glossary provides a fun way for students to match words with their definitions, helping to learn key vocabulary and ideas.

COMMERCIAL BREAK

How about developing the advertisements from the commercial break with extra jingles, cheesy ad-talk, dialogue, sketches, slogans and even a few puppets thrown in the mix?

Index

B

Bellamy, Samuel 4, 14–15, 22, 52–53, 97–102, 109, 162

Blackbeard 4, 13, 15, 17–18, 22–26, 33–37, 39–40, 43–44, 47, 50, 57, 63–69, 71, 84, 86–89, 92–102, 109–116, 119, 151–153, 155–156, 158, 162

Bonny, Anne 4, 73, 75, 134, 139–140, 145–149, 162

E

Every, Henry 153, 161

H

Hornigold, Captain Benjamin 4, 15, 46, 53, 98, 109–111, 113

K

Kidd, Captain 4, 121–127, 152, 162

Killigrew, Lady 4, 134–138, 140, 161

M

Maynard, Captain Robert 4, 63–71, 84, 87–88, 94, 111, 162

Morgan, Henry 4, 134, 142–144

R

Rackham, Jack 4, 73, 134, 139, 144–148, 162

Read, Mary 4, 72–75, 134, 139–141, 145, 147–148, 162

Roberts, Bartholomew 114–119, 162

S

Shih, Ching 128–131, 163

W

Wall, Rachel 4, 134–136, 138, 144, 147–148